KS2 HISTORY IS EASY

ANGLO-SAXONS AND SCOTS

www.How2Become.com

As part of this product you have also received FREE access to online tests that will help you to pass History (Anglo-Saxons and Scots) for KS1 and KS2.

To gain access, simply go to:

www.MyEducationalTests.co.uk

Get more products for passing any test at:

www.How2Become.com

Orders: Please contact How2Become Ltd, Suite 1, 60 Churchill Square Business Centre, Kings Hill, Kent ME19 4YU.

You can order through Amazon.co.uk under ISBN: 9781911259114, via the website www.How2Become.com or through Gardners.com.

ISBN: 9781911259114

First published in 2017 by How2Become Ltd.

Typeset by Gemma Butler for How2Become Ltd.

Disclaimer

Every effort has been made to ensure that the information contained within this guide is accurate at the time of publication. How2Become Ltd is not responsible for anyone failing any part of any selection process as a result of the information contained within this guide. How2Become Ltd and their authors cannot accept any responsibility for any errors or omissions within this guide, however caused. No responsibility for loss or damage occasioned by any person acting, or refraining from action, as a result of the material in this publication can be accepted by How2Become Ltd.

The information within this guide does not represent the views of any third-party service or organisation.

Contents

THE NEW NATIONAL
CURRICULUM
(GUIDANCE FOR PARENTS)

WHY CHILDREN ARE TAUGHT HISTORY IN SCHOOLS

History is a part of the primary syllabus. Studying history gives children an introduction to the major events which have shaped Britain, and provides them with a better understanding of historical global relations. The aim of the subject is to inspire a deeper curiosity for how society has changed over the course of time.

WHAT ARE THE AIMS OF THE HISTORY SYLLABUS?

The syllabus provides children with:

- An understanding of British history as a chronological narrative, from ancient times to the present day. It focuses on how British people have been influenced by the rest of the world, and how they have made their own influence felt.

- An understanding of the essential events and features of the history of the world as a whole, focusing on the earliest civilisations, most powerful empires, and the ways in which humanity has succeeded and failed.

- A wide historical vocabulary and an understanding of key terms and concepts such as 'civilisation' and 'society'.

- An introduction to wider historical concepts such as: continuity and change, cause and consequence, similarity, difference, and significance, and how to use them to make connections, draw contrasts, analyse trends, frame historically valid questions, and create their own structured accounts, including written narratives and analysis.

- An understanding of the importance of evidence when putting forward historical opinions. This also includes thinking about why some people interpret events or facts differently.

- An introduction to historical perspective, by considering contexts such as location, economics, politics, religion, and key points in time.

Key Stage 1

Below we have outlined specific criteria that should be considered when studying History at Key Stage 1.

Pupils should:

- Develop an awareness of the past, using common words and phrases to describe the passage of time.

- Know where the people and events they study fit within a chronological framework, and identify similarities and differences between ways of life in different periods.

- Use a wide vocabulary of everyday historical terms.

- Ask and answer questions, choosing and using parts of stories and other sources to show that they know and understand key features of events.

- Understand some of the ways in which we find out about the past, and identify different ways in which the past is represented.

Key focuses

- Changes in national life within living memory.

- Historical events beyond living memory, with national and/or international significance.

- The lives of individuals who have contributed significant achievements.

Key Stage 2

Below we have outlined specific criteria that should be considered when studying History at Key Stage 2.

Pupils should:

- Continue to develop a chronologically secure knowledge and understanding of local, British, and world history.

- Establish clear narratives within and across the studied historical periods.

- Note connections, contrasts, and trends over time and develop the appropriate use of historical terms.

- Address questions about change, cause, similarity, difference, and significance.

- Construct informed responses that involve thoughtful selection and organisation of relevant historical information.

- Understand how our knowledge of the past is constructed from a range of sources.

Key focuses

- Changes in Britain from the Stone Age to the Iron Age.

- The Roman Empire and its impact on Britain.

- Britain's settlement by Anglo-Saxons and Scots.

- The Viking and Anglo-Saxon struggle for the Kingdom of England, up to the time of Edward the Confessor.

- A local history study (this will of course vary from school to school.)

- A study of an aspect or theme in British history that extends pupils' chronological knowledge beyond 1066. (E.g. the changing power of monarchs – using case studies such as John, Anne, and Victoria.)

- The achievements of the earliest civilisations, such as Ancient Egypt or Ancient China.

- Ancient Greece, its achievements, and its influence on the western world.

- A non-European society that provides contrasts with British history, such as early Islamic civilisation, or the Mayan civilisation.

BRITAIN BEFORE THE ANGLO-SAXONS

BRITAIN BEFORE THE ANGLO-SAXONS

The Anglo-Saxon Age in Britain began around the year 400, and lasted for over 600 years. But, before we look at who the Anglo-Saxons were, it is important to get an idea of what Britain was like before they arrived! In the years before the Anglo-Saxon Age, Britain had been under the control of the Roman Empire for centuries, and had gone through massive change as a result.

So, let's look at how the Romans lost power in Western Europe, and what state they had left it in!

Roman Britain

A fallen Empire

The Dark Ages

Okay, we'll leave!

Join our defeated Roman soldier, Atticus, as we begin looking at this topic!

ROMAN BRITAIN

The Romans had a huge impact on Britain, turning England from a collection of separate tribes into a nation of Britons with productive cities and wealth. The Romans were in Britain for nearly 400 years, from around the year 40 to the year 400.

This period is known as the Roman Age in Britain.

During this time, Britain and its people went through many changes. Below is a summary of these, looking at people's use of **language**, how **culture** developed, Britain's **government** (how it was ruled), and how **technology and architecture** were improved.

LANGUAGE	Britons began to learn how to read, write and count. They also adopted the Roman calendar, which is very similar to the one we use today.
CULTURE	Britons were introduced to **Christianity** by the Romans. Also, the Romans introduced their style of **art**, **poems**, and **buildings** to the Britons.
GOVERNMENT	Concepts of **democracy** (voting) and **nationhood** were introduced.
TECHNOLOGY AND ARCHITECTURE	The first British **roads** were built by the Romans, giving rise to the first British **towns**. Also, the Romans built aqueducts, drains, and sewers in Britain – people now had **toilets** and **running water**.

So, as you can see, the Romans had a hand in developing nearly every aspect of life possible in Britain. Most importantly though, the Romans changed who the people in Britain were. During the Roman era, Celtic people and the Romans began to mix, resulting in a nation of new Romano-Britons.

But, the Romans did eventually have to let go of their claim on Britain. Keep reading to find out what this meant for its people!

A FALLEN EMPIRE

So, now you know how the Romans changed Britain, you might be wondering why they left (around the year 400). There is no simple answer to this question; there are many factors to consider. In the end, the Romans had no choice.

By this time, the Roman Empire spanned huge amounts of the world, including most of Western and Central Europe, as well as large parts of North Africa and the Middle East. Rome was its capital, and governors took control of the different regions across the Empire.

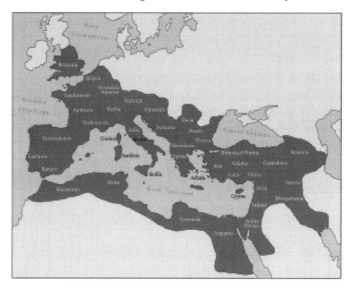

As you can imagine, it took a lot of hard work to govern such a large area. This included paying more and more soldiers, as the area they controlled got bigger and bigger. Eventually, this area got too big, and the Romans struggled to deal with attacks from bands of tribesmen like the Huns, whom they called barbarians.

The Romans' power in Western Europe seemed to be crumbling, so they made the decision to flee the area and focus on their land in the East, where their position was more stable. This meant that Roman leaders and soldiers left Britain, leaving its new population defenceless against the tribesmen.

Britain was left alone with no army or leaders!

THE DARK AGES

So, what did this mean for Britain and its people? Although the Romans had been responsible for so much change, much of the Roman culture in Britain was lost once the Roman leaders left.

Soon, Western Europe would enter the Dark Ages – a period of history where general progress was slow, and very little seems to have been written down. This is due to the fact that the major historians of the time (the people writing down what was going on) were mostly Roman.

So, when they left Britain, there were very few people recording the events of the time. We can say that the Dark Ages lasted from around the year 400 to the year 600.

> **This is why we do not know much about what actually happened!**

The Barbarians in Western Europe

The Dark Ages were also related to the activity of the tribesmen who had the Romans running scared at this time. We know that tribesmen raids led to the destruction of towns and cities, which caused the Romans to leave Britain. But who were these tribes, and where did they come from?

We can say that most of them were **nomadic** tribes. This meant that they did not have a permanent home or a country they were loyal to, at least at the time of the first raids.

They belonged to separate groups, who travelled around raiding towns and cities for gold. Major tribes of this time included **the Huns**, who came from Asia, and **the Vandals** and **Goths**, who came from parts of Europe outside of Roman control.

In their invasions across the Roman Empire, they would burn cities down and rob them of their riches. They also began to take back land that the Romans had previously taken from them.

Attila the Hun

Perhaps the most famous of these warring tribesmen is Attila the Hun. The Huns were responsible for several attacks on the Roman Empire over many years, as well as becoming the dominant tribe in Europe after invading from Asia. They were widely feared across these areas, known for their ruthless fighting style.

According to Roman historians, the Huns were such good fighters due to their incredible ability on horseback. They were experts at combing long-range archery (while still riding!), with short-range charges with swords.

In terms of strategy, the Huns excelled at using the element of surprise. They would swarm enemies with extreme speed and often win before the enemy knew what hit them. What's more, the Huns were known for their sheer bravery – they showed no fear during battle.

Unfairly Represented?

However, the tribes were far more than their raids across Europe. Although not as advanced as the Romans in terms of building, culture, and education, many people today believe that they were no more savage or bloody than the so-called sophisticated Romans.

But, during the time of the attacks and raids, Roman writers and artists would create work that presented the tribesmen in a devil-like light. For example, paintings were made of Attila the Hun with devil horns.

> **What reason could they have to write about the tribesmen in this way?**

Roman historians have provided us with excellent insights into the tribes and how they fought. However, it is important to think about how their descriptions of the tribes might be unfair or inaccurate. Consider the fact that the Romans were among the only people recording history in Europe at the time; we do not have a fair range of sources discussing the tribesmen.

A primary source: writing or drawing that was created at the point in time you are studying. This gives us lots of information about whatever we are learning about.

We only have one, biased history of the tribesmen to consider when talking about them. The tribes were responsible for destroying Roman cities, and made up a big part of why the Empire began to lose control of Europe. How would this affect writings about people like Attila the Hun?

Question Time!

QUESTION 1

How was Britain's new population of Romano-Britons created?

_____

_____

_____

QUESTION 2

Using the bullet points below, write down two reasons why the Romans left Western Europe to focus on their land in Eastern Europe.

• _____

• _____

QUESTION 3

What was the Huns' main reason for attacking the Roman Empire?

_____

QUESTION 4

Answer the following questions by circling either 'True' or 'False' for each one.

I. Europe made a lot of progress during the Dark Ages.

TRUE   **FALSE**

II. Britain was left in a weak position when the Roman Army stopped protecting it.

TRUE   **FALSE**

III. It is difficult for us to know what was going on during the Dark Ages, because there weren't many people recording its events.

TRUE   **FALSE**

QUESTION 5

The box below is filled with words to do with the Huns and their fighting style. Use them to fill the gaps in the paragraph underneath.

		swords
arrows		
	horses	
range		

The Huns were extremely good at fighting while riding

_____, and they could even hit targets with

_____ while doing so. In addition to this, the Huns

were devastating attackers at close _____. They

would swarm over enemies and cause frightening damage with their

_____.

QUESTION 6

Why is it likely that the Roman writings of the time would present the tribespeople in a bad light?

_____

_____

_____

_____

Answers

QUESTION 1

Britain's new population was created following the mixing of the Romans and the Celtic Britons over many years.

QUESTION 2

Two reasons why the Romans left Western Europe:

- They found themselves in control of too much land; their army could no longer protect all of the Empire.

- Invading tribesmen like the Huns were destroying towns and killing many people in this area.

QUESTION 3

The Huns' main reason for attacking the Roman Empire was to steal their gold!

QUESTION 4

I. Europe made a lot of progress during the dark ages: **FALSE**.

II. Britain was left in a weak position when the Roman Army stopped protecting it: **TRUE**.

III. It is difficult for us to know what was going on during the Dark Ages, because there weren't many people recording its events: **TRUE**.

QUESTION 5

The completed paragraph:

The Huns were extremely good at fighting while riding **horses**, and could even hit targets with **arrows** while doing so. In addition to this, the Huns were devastating at close **range**. They would swarm over enemies and cause frightening damage with their **swords**.

QUESTION 6

It is likely that the Roman writings of the time would present the tribespeople in a bad light because they were a big reason that they lost control of Western Europe. This means that the Romans would have been upset with the Huns. Also, the Huns killed many people and destroyed many cities by burning them down.

THE ANGLES AND SAXONS

THE ANGLES AND SAXONS

In this chapter, we will look at what happened next for Britain. Firstly, we will explore what state Britain was in when new tribal invaders, the Angles and Saxons, came to visit. We will also look at the motives of these new players at this time, as well as how they were able to take Britain for themselves. How were the Angles and Saxons able to gain control of Britain, and why did they want to move away from their homeland? Read on to find out.

The state of post-Roman Britain

The Scots and Picts

Saxon treachery

The Anglo-Saxons take control

We are the Britons now!

The Saxon warrior Aldwyn, will guide you through this section!

THE STATE OF POST-ROMAN BRITAIN

After reading the previous chapter, it might be difficult to imagine what life in Britain was actually like just after the Romans left. As previously mentioned, the lack of writing that took place at this time has left us with a murky view of these years.

However, there were some who were determined to record the history of this time. In around the year 500, a historian monk called Gildas began writing about the events of the previous 100 years. From this source, we are able to build up an idea of what happened in Britain after the Romans left.

See below for a timeline of events from Gildas's point of view, with some quotes from the writing itself.

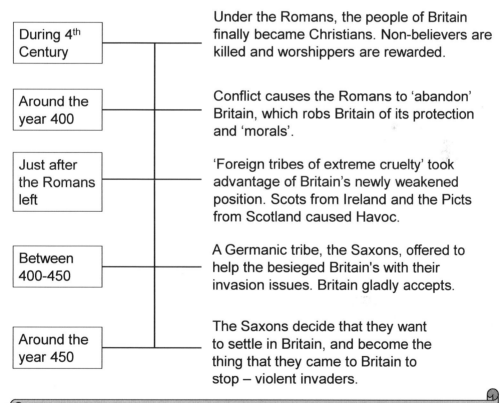

During 4th Century	Under the Romans, the people of Britain finally became Christians. Non-believers are killed and worshippers are rewarded.
Around the year 400	Conflict causes the Romans to 'abandon' Britain, which robs Britain of its protection and 'morals'.
Just after the Romans left	'Foreign tribes of extreme cruelty' took advantage of Britain's newly weakened position. Scots from Ireland and the Picts from Scotland caused Havoc.
Between 400-450	A Germanic tribe, the Saxons, offered to help the besieged Britain's with their invasion issues. Britain gladly accepts.
Around the year 450	The Saxons decide that they want to settle in Britain, and become the thing that they came to Britain to stop – violent invaders.

Start to think about Gildas's different feeling towards the Romans and tribes like the Picts.

Discussion of Gildas's work

As a monk, Gildas was mostly concerned with writing about the state of Christianity during this time. While this might seem to be a limited view of events at this time, the Christian religion was an extremely important part of European society. So, Gildas's writings give us a valuable insight into events around the time of the first Saxon invasions of Britain.

Glastonbury Abbey (as seen today), where there was a shrine to Gildas before its destruction in the 1600s by Henry VIII.

However, it is possible to say that Gildas's writing was too emotional and biased, not presenting a clear view of events. Importantly, Gildas's most famous writing about the events surrounding the Romans leaving Britain is called '***De Excidio et Conquestu Britanniae***' which means '***On the Ruin and Conquest of Britain***'.

Gildas was Roman Catholic – how do you think he felt about the Romans leaving?

Immediately, you can tell that Gildas sees the events as a very bad thing for Britain. The title of his work shows us that he is not interested in presenting a balanced, fact-based story. Rather, he is writing to put forward a strong and passionate opinion. This means we should be careful about how much of his version of events we can accept as fact.

The Venerable Bede

Another important historian who wrote about this time was called Bede. Also a monk, Bede was writing around 200 years after Gildas, which meant he could use Gildas's work for research, as well as other sources. Bede was special because he was one of the first historians to look at many different sources to try and work out what happened in the past. Of course, this is still how historians work today.

> Looking at both primary sources AND previous historians' writing will give you the best insight into a historical event.

As a monk, Bede still looked at events from a Christian view, but his writing was much less passionate and much more professional than that of Gildas. It is for this reason that he has come to be known as 'Venerable', which means 'well-respected'. This title is also a holy one given by the Catholic Church – it is not far from sainthood.

Bede's most famous work, *The Ecclesiastical History of the English People* is a hugely detailed study of Britain and its journey towards Christianity. For its time, it was an incredible achievement, because Bede was writing about events around 700 years before he was born. This was much more difficult than it would be for someone today, due to the lack of resources that Bede would have had available to him.

This incredible work has caused many to call him 'the father of English history'.

THE SCOTS AND THE PICTS

Now that we have looked at who was writing about Britain around the time the Romans left, let's change our focus back to the events themselves! As Gildas wrote, people in Britain soon found themselves the victims of attacks from the Scots, who came from what is now called Ireland, and the Picts, who came from what is now called Scotland.

You'll notice that (confusingly) the Scots did not come from Scotland – it was not called that at the time.

Raiding and invading

The Scots and Picts would have known that the Roman Army was no longer in place to protect Britain from their invasions. As mentioned before, we do not have a clear idea as to what the Scots and Picts wanted to get out of carrying out such attacks – we only have Gildas's writing to go on. Gildas presented the tribesmen as being like animals, describing them as a 'barbarian horde', 'wolves', and even 'worms'.

According to Gildas, the raids from these tribes went on unopposed until the Britons actually asked the Romans for help. After that, the Romans were said to have returned to Britain's aid, and driven the Picts and Scots away. The Romans then armed the Britons, and helped them set up defences. They then set off back to Rome, never to return.

However, this was not the last the Britons were to hear of the warring tribes. Gildas goes on to say that the Picts and Scots started raiding again almost immediately after the Romans left for the second and final time. This time, the tribesmen started to take land for themselves and settled in Britain.

By this point, Gildas seems to suggest that the Britons found their fighting ability, and managed to gain a victory from the previously dominant Picts. Even better, Gildas goes on to explain the newfound wealth that people in Britain found at this time after the period of peace. However, Gildas also makes his displeasure known about the amount of sin that he saw happening, even writing about a great plague sent by God to punish Britain.

The plague was not to be the end of the Britons' troubles; the Scots had set up homes (where Scotland is now!) and were continuing to raid and plunder, to the great anguish of the Britons.

The Britons found themselves needing help again. Enter the Anglo-Saxons...

SAXON TREACHARY

According to legend, Britain soon turned to outside help once again; the Picts and Scots were still terrorising settlements in the north of the country. Here, 'legend' means a tale that was passed through spoken word across many generations; there is not much archaeological evidence for any of these events at this time.

So, a British king named Vortigern asked three Germanic tribes (the Angles, Saxons, and Jutes) to sail to Britain to help fight off the Picts and Scots. They accepted, as Vortigern promised the payment of gold and land. He knew that these new tribes had many good fighters, who had the ability to bring peace to Britain.

Indeed, these new allies were able to drive the Picts and Scots away. According to Gildas, the Britons were pathetically grateful, as well as pathetic generally.

The Saxons saw this as well, and soon decided that they wanted more money and more land than they had already been given. So, they set about taking it by force, and became more violent and brutal than the people they had come over to protect the British from.

> But, some historians doubt Gildas's version of events, since his motive for writing was to spread fear about what would happen if Britons did not obey God!

Myth and legend

Since we do not know exactly what went on around the year 500 (only that Anglo-Saxons began to settle in Britain) there are also many myths and legends about the time following this supposed betrayal. This is partly because people in Britain wanted to create a culture and history for themselves.

One Anglo-Saxon legend concerns two warrior brothers called Hengist and Horsa, two of the new foreign warriors that Vortigern was said to have hired to fight the Scots and Picts. Supposedly, they were extraordinary fighters who gained many victories for Vortigern and the Britons.

But, they were part of the Anglo-Saxon forces who later betrayed the Britons, and began fighting them with the aim of taking their wealth and land. According to the Venerable Bede, Horsa was killed during one of their campaigns against the Britons. Meanwhile, Hengist went on to become one of the first Anglo-Saxon kings in England, ruling the county of Kent for the Jutes.

King Arthur

However, the downtrodden Britons had legends of their own. Unsurprisingly, these legends were all of heroic British warriors who stood up to the treachery of the Anglo-Saxons. The most famous of these from around the year 500 is that of King Arthur.

There are many stories that people tell about King Arthur. You've probably heard of the one involving the Knights of the Round Table, the sword and the stone, and a wizard named Merlin. However, there are a few stories about King Arthur that are a bit more believable.

For example, around the year 500, there was said to have been a great clash between the Britons and the Anglo-Saxons called the Battle of Badon. According to some, it was a great warrior named Arthur who won the day, defeating the invading tribesman almost single-handedly.

It is difficult to trust this story because it was told around 200 years after the battle was supposed to have happened – no one told this story at the time!

THE ANGLO-SAXONS TAKE CONTROL

Despite the stories that the British told about their successes in fighting back against the Anglo-Saxons, it is certain that they were eventually defeated. As a result, the Anglo-Saxons began to take over the whole island. Before too long, most of England and Wales would be under their control.

> We have a better idea of what was happening from around the year 550, because there were people writing about their own time, something that hadn't happened in Britain since the Romans left!

The first areas of Britain that were taken over by the Anglo-Saxons were the East and South East of England. The Jutes claimed Kent, while the Saxons claimed most of the rest of the South East. It was the Angles who settled in a huge portion of Eastern England, as well as much of the Midlands. After this, they started to move further and further west.

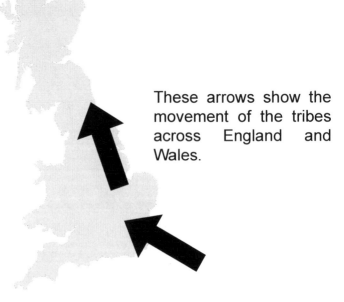

These arrows show the movement of the tribes across England and Wales.

Meanwhile, the Scots and Picts continued to control areas of Scotland, while Britons still controlled areas of Eastern England. However, the amount of land held by the British was constantly shrinking as time went on.

The Birth of Kingdoms

At this point, the Jutes, Angles, and Saxons were still not a unified people. This meant that they settled separately, and stuck with their own. These separate settlements eventually came to be known as kingdoms. They had their own leaders, laws, and differing ways of life and culture.

Over time, they began to collectively be referred to as the Anglo-Saxons; although the tradition of separate kingdoms did not come to an end. In fact, the Angles, Saxons, and Jutes eventually split up further, creating several new kingdoms with different names.

- **Angles**: Split up to form the kingdoms of East Anglia, Mercia, and Northumbria.

- **Saxons**: Split up to form the kingdoms of Essex, Middlesex, Sussex, and Wessex.

- **Jutes**: Formed the kingdom of Cantaware (Kent), and other small settlements.

Why did they want to settle in Britain?

As we have discussed, we do not have a clear idea of what actually happened when the Anglo-Saxons first arrived in Britain. As a result, we do not have a clear understanding of the reasons for them wanting to live here!

However, historians have come up with a few reasons for why they may have wanted to leave their central European homes. The most compelling of which is all to do with farming.

Historians believe that the low-lying farmlands in central Europe were easily flooded when it rained. This made growing food more difficult. This was not as big of a problem in Britain, so the fertile farmlands would have appealed to visiting Anglo-Saxons.

It is also possible that some tribespeople's reasons for settling in Britain were more simple. If the Britons did ask the Anglo-Saxons for help fighting against the Scots and Picts (as Gildas said), then it is possible that they did so, and afterwards simply chose not to return home.

Question Time!

QUESTION 1

Using the timeline on page 25, pick out some words that Gildas uses to show his:

a) Bitterness towards the Romans for leaving Britain:

b) Disgust at the Picts and Scots invading:

QUESTION 2

In one sentence, write down what reason you think Gildas (as a monk) might have to describe the Scots and Picts as being like a plague.

QUESTION 3

Answer the following multiple-choice questions by choosing either **a)**, **b)** or **c)**:

I. Why is Bede generally considered to be a more reliable historian than Gildas?

a) Bede looked at sources from the time he lived, as well as very old sources when writing.

b) Bede was more important to the Catholic Church.

c) Gildas moved to France, while Bede stayed in Britain his whole life.

II. Why did the attacking Scots not come from what we now call Scotland?

a) At the time, what we now call Scotland was not called Scotland.

b) The Scots did not live in what is now called Scotland at this time.

c) Both of the above.

III. Why did the Romans return to Britain soon after the Scots and Picts attacked?

a) They had become strong in Western Europe again and wanted Britain back.

b) Their soldiers were out of practice and wanted a fight.

c) The Britons begged them to fight on their behalf and get rid of the Picts and Scots.

IV. What were the results of the time of peace following the above events?

    a) The British people built one of the strongest armies in the world.

    b) The British people became wealthy.

    c) The British were never invaded again.

QUESTION 4

In what way do Hengist and Horsa represent early Anglo-Saxon dealings with Britain?

_____

_____

_____

_____

QUESTION 5

Write about why you think people would tell stories such as those to do with King Arthur. There are no wrong answers to this question; write your own opinion!

_____

_____

_____

_____

QUESTION 6

In the spaces below, complete the labelling of the map showing where the different groups of people were most powerful in England and Wales (around the year 550). The names of these groups in the box below. The first one has been done for you.

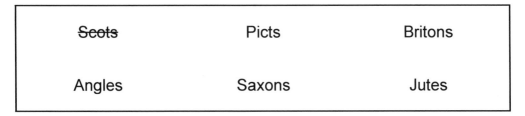

~~Scots~~	Picts	Britons
Angles	Saxons	Jutes

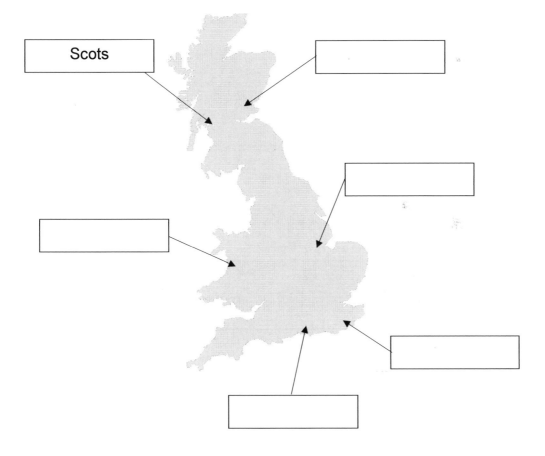

Scots

QUESTION 7

In the table below, sort the new Anglo-Saxon kingdoms (shown in the boxes) into the three headings of '**Angles**', '**Saxons**', and '**Jutes**', based on which tribes they originated from.

| Wessex |
| Northumbria |
| Sussex |

| Cantaware |
| Mercia |

| Essex |
| Middlesex |
| East Anglia |

Angles	Saxons	Jutes

QUESTION 8

Why was farmland in Britain more ideal than farmland in Central Europe?

_____

_____

_____

Answers

QUESTION 1

a) Gildas shows his bitterness at the Romans leaving Britain with words like 'abandon'. He also writes about how Britain lost its 'morals' as a result.

b) Gildas shows his disgust at the Picts and Scots invading by describing them as 'tribes of extreme cruelty'.

QUESTION 2

Gildas might have described the Scots and Picts being like a plague upon Britain, to express his view that the invasions were a punishment from God; Gildas felt that people in Britain were not holy enough.

QUESTION 3

I. Why is Bede generally considered to be a more reliable historian than Gildas?

   a) Bede looked at sources from the time he lived in, as well as very old sources when writing.

II. Why did the attacking Scots not come from what we now call Scotland?

   c) Both of the above.

III. Why did the Romans return to Britain soon after the Scots and Picts attacked?

   c) The Britons begged them to fight on their behalf and get rid of the Picts and Scots.

IV. What were the results of the time of peace following the above events?

b) The British people became wealthy.

QUESTION 4

Hengist and Horsa represent early Anglo-Saxon dealings with Britain, because they were said to have travelled to Britain from mainland Europe to help fight the Picts and Scots. Also, they soon turned on the Britons, fighting them and taking their land.

QUESTION 5

(This answer is based on personal opinion, but see below for a sample response)

I think that people create legends like King Arthur in order to create a culture for themselves. They could also draw on such stories for inspiration in times of hardship, or before an important battle.

QUESTION 6

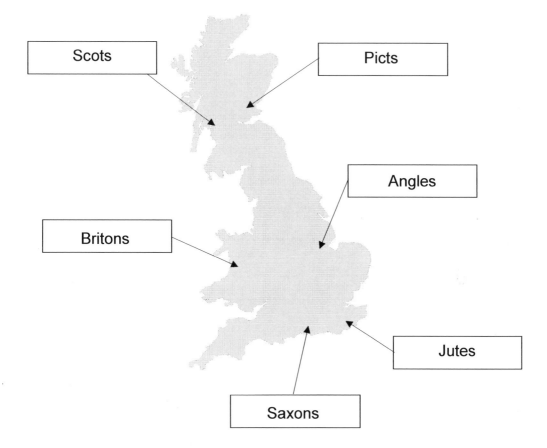

QUESTION 7

Angles	Saxons	Jutes
East Anglia	Essex	Cantaware
Mercia	Middlesex	
Northumbria	Sussex	
	Wessex	

QUESTION 8

Farmland in Britain was more ideal than farmland in Central Europe, because it was less prone to flooding.

ANGLO-SAXON BRITAIN

ANGLO-SAXON BRITAIN

Now we have looked at the time just before and during the Anglo-Saxon takeover of Britain, our focus will change to what came next for Britain. Life would begin to change for people in Anglo-Saxon Britain – everyday life and culture began to move away from what it was like during the Roman Era, with a new set of values and traditions being adopted. So, what were the details of all this change? Find out in this chapter.

Anglo-Saxon society

Civil war

Anglo-Saxon culture

Try to get rid of us now!

Our Mercian thane, Ceolwulf, is on hand with his knowledge and strength!

ANGLO-SAXON SOCIETY

Anglo-Saxon settlements

Using archaeological evidence, historians have been able to paint us a picture of what Anglo-Saxon villages and towns would have looked like around 1500 years ago. This even includes letting us know what the buildings themselves would have looked like.

> **Archaeological evidence refers to ancient remains that can tell us what something was like many years ago.**

Anglo-Saxons nearly always built their houses out of wood, and used straw to thatch their rooves. In an Anglo-Saxon settlement, it would usually be one family to a house, who would all sleep, cook, and eat in one room.

The room would be heated by an open fire which was located in the centre of the house. This was also how the Anglo-Saxons would cook their vegetables and meat. Most Anglo-Saxons did not have beds as we know them now, and slept on little more than cloth-covered benches either side of the fire.

Also, the farm animals belonging to a family would share their house, kept in a small pen that was half inside and half outside. Look at the left side of the picture on the previous page for an idea of what this would look like.

What did Anglo-Saxons do?

Anglo-Saxon life was dominated by farming. Children of all ages would help out as much as they could – there was not much focus on education, or even much of a concept of 'childhood' at all. In other words, children were not generally given the amount of help and support that they get today – they were considered as being on the same level as adults from a very young age. Children would herd cattle, help plant vegetables, and keep an eye out for predators like wolves, who wanted to eat their sheep.

The Anglo-Saxons were also very good at building and crafting. Blacksmiths would create tools and weapons, potters would work with clay, and jewellers would craft beautiful golden jewellery. Of course, settlements would also need hunters and soldiers. Clearly, life was tough for Anglo-Saxons, who had to work hard just to survive.

Anglo-Saxon Religion

At the time the Anglo-Saxons came to England, they were Pagans. This meant that they were not yet Christians, and believed in many gods, and celebrated Pagan festivals. The many different gods would represent many different things. For example, the early Anglo-Saxons worshipped a god of thunder, Thunor, who was very similar to the Norse god, Thor. In fact, the early Anglo-Saxons lived very similar lives to the early Vikings. Also, praying to a particular god was said to bring people luck in that area. For example, if you wanted good luck in battle, you would pray to the war god, Tiw.

However, the Anglo-Saxons eventually made the move to Christianity. The first Anglo-Saxon king to convert was King Ethelbert of Kent around the year 600. Christianity soon became an important part of people's lives. Monasteries and churches were built up and down Britain, and became a vital part of society. They not only became centres for spirituality but also for education; nearly all writing that came out of the Anglo-Saxon era was done by monks and religious figures.

The make-up of society

In terms of daily life, most families would own just enough land to be able to grow and rear their own food, and live alongside each other in villages.

However, rich Anglo-Saxons were able to have bigger houses, own more land, and wield more power in settlements and villages. Eventually, the most powerful men in these settlements declared themselves as kings, turning the settlements into kingdoms. More often than not, the king was the best fighter in the area, as this was how he earned the kingship. However, a king would face frequent threats to his authority, sometimes having to fight challengers for power.

Early Anglo-Saxon villages would also be home to a class of people called Thanes. Thanes owned more land than most, had bigger houses and were generally richer. Similarly to how the kings gained power, people generally became Thanes due to the fact that they could fight.

Kings would have favourite Thanes who made up personal armies for them. As you'll discover in the next section, loyalty was extremely important for Anglo-Saxons. In any case, it was a good idea to have loyal fighters, as local kings would often fight with each other over land and wealth.

Anglo-Saxon Women

Gender was also very important in Anglo-Saxon society. Women were expected to carry out the will of the men. This meant that they had to do the bulk of the household tasks. This included weaving material to make clothes and looking after children.

What's more, women were regularly forced to marry people they had never met, in order to secure alliances or to finalise trade deals. It was rare for a woman to rise up to wield any real power. Having said this, Anglo-Saxon women were able to own land, and get divorced in certain situations.

Soldier status

Most Anglo-Saxon soldiers only had simple battle equipment. Weapons were light but powerful, and protection was fairly limited. Look at the picture below to see what they looked like.

However, the richest and most powerful Anglo-Saxons could afford to have iron longswords. As a result, swords were a status symbol of the upper classes and the best fighters. The wealthy often decorated their swords, coating the handles with gold or studding them with jewels.

Iron helmet

Iron battle-axe (or spear)

Round shields

ANGLO-SAXON CULTURE

We have also been able to discover how Anglo-Saxons liked to spend their free time, and what hobbies they had. An example of this is the fact that the Anglo-Saxons were master craftsmen. We know this as we have found buried treasure from their time period.

Also, Anglo-Saxon soldiers loved drinking mead and feasting together in large halls, often called the 'Great Hall' of a settlement. Here, they would be entertained by poets and bards, who often spoke and sang of great battles, warriors and leaders of the past. To be immortalised in song like this was a great honour, and would have been something that leaders of the time had in mind and perhaps even aimed for.

The Anglo-Saxons also wrote down their tales and stories; Anglo-Saxon literature (writing) was some of the first to come out of Britain. We can point to great works such as Beowulf, an epic poem (written between the years 700-900) as a surviving classic from this era. People still read and enjoy this story today – it was even made into a Hollywood film.

Loyalty and roles

A very important part of Anglo-Saxon culture has to do with their attitude to war. The Anglo-Saxons believed that it was incredibly important to give their all for their leader. This concept of loyalty between soldiers and their leaders was vital for an Anglo-Saxon; they had a near-sacred bond. Breaking such a bond by betraying a leader, or even showing cowardice in battle, was about the worst thing an Anglo-Saxon could do. Furthermore, Anglo-Saxon kings would have favourite Thanes, on whom they would bestow gifts and land, by way of thanking them for their loyalty.

Clearly, this sense of hierarchy (everyone having a rank and a place) was very important in Anglo-Saxon society. Violence formed part of the Anglo-Saxon justice system – disputes were often settled with fights. Men would also fight for their king in campaigns against other kings.

This is also how Anglo-Saxon law was carried out; criminals would be judged by the community and exiled, or even killed.

Anglo-Saxon gold

Over the years, archaeologists have found lots of evidence of how the Anglo-Saxons lived their lives. The treasures that they buried give us an insight into what they owned and what importance their possessions had.

One of the best archaeological finds in British history occurred at Sutton Hoo, Suffolk, in 1939.

The Sutton Hoo burial

Archaeologists were drawn to undisturbed Anglo-Saxon burial mounds that were located near a river in Sutton Hoo. They began to explore the largest one, and were amazed at what they discovered.

They found the remains of a huge Viking longship, which was filled with untold treasures and riches. For example, there was an iron sword complete with a gold handle, a battle shield, and many bowls made of bronze and silver. Not only that, but buried beneath the mound was an ornate purse filled with gold coins and an extremely valuable golden belt buckle.

However, the highlight of this incredible find was a beautifully decorated and detailed iron helmet.

The investigators soon confirmed that it was an Anglo-Saxon grave.

CONCLUSIONS WE CAN MAKE ABOUT WHO WAS BURIED HERE

- The sword shows us the grave belonged to a great warrior – swords were a very important symbol of leadership for the Anglo-Saxons. Not every soldier was in a position to own one.

- The lavish dining bowls and the massive purse filled with gold show us that the person who was buried here was extremely rich.

- The extravagant iron helmet shows he was a leader. In fact, this grave almost certainly belonged to a king. The helmet was designed to convey power and wealth, with a very masculine design. It even has a moustache!

- The items found in this grave show us the Anglo-Saxon view of the afterlife. Being buried in a boat was said to aid entrance into heaven, being buried with weapons helped them to be better prepared for the afterlife, and the gold was there to help them pay their way in the next life.

The Anglo-Saxon Chronicle

One of the most important and informative examples of this Anglo-Saxon written tradition is the Anglo-Saxon Chronicle.

It is a huge document, written over hundreds of years by several Anglo-Saxon historians in order to record the events of their time. First ordered by Alfred the Great (see page 83 for more), it represents a hugely valuable historical source that has provided us with huge amounts of information about what England was like between the years 890 and 1150.

The Anglo-Saxon Chronicle is the main reason we know so much about when certain kings lived or where battles took place!

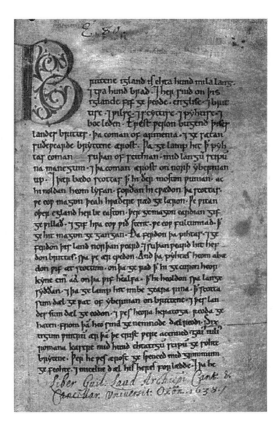

Alfred the Great was responsible for ordering this document to be created, and it even aimed to recount history that had happened in the decades before the 9th century.

The kingdoms within Anglo-Saxon Britain were nearly always in conflict – fighting each other for control of people and land. For an idea of what a map of Britain would look like at around the year 800, look at the image below. As you can see, by this time the Anglo-Saxons had taken over the vast majority of England, with the native Britons only holding on to Scotland and Wales.

CIVIL WAR

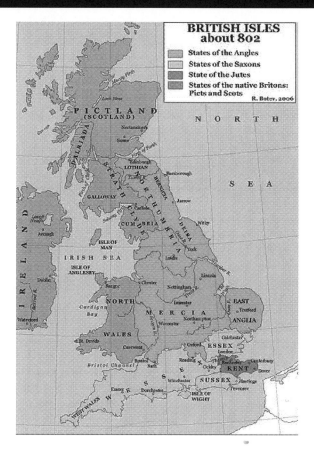

As you can see, the Angles' kingdom of Mercia was the largest and most dominant in Britain at the time. Historians have decided that this was partly down to the leadership and skill of the great warrior king Offa.

King Offa of Mercia

Offa was born around the year 730, becoming king in 757 after the death of his cousin. Due to the fact that it was not just him who wanted the throne, Offa had to defeat a rival, named Beornred, in a series of battles in the year 757. This tells us that even before his kingship started, he had proven his leadership qualities and shown his strength in battle.

Mercia was large even before Offa began to expand its borders, and it had a central location in the country. This put Offa in a favourable position even before he started making moves to increase Mercia's power.

One of the first of these moves involved Offa turning his attention towards the South. During the time in which Offa came to the throne, Kent (south-eastern England) was going through a time of uncertainty – many people were all competing for control of the area. Offa used this to his advantage, swooping in and proclaiming himself overlord.

He was probably able to do this because people in Kent were intimidated by his army. Some will have even have welcomed Offa, hoping he would bring stability and peace. However, it is not clear if this really happened or not.

Offa also worked to protect the Mercian border to the West – he took steps to mark out his own territory from that of the Welsh. He did this by constructing what came to be known as 'Offa's Dyke'.

Offa's Dyke is a huge man-made trench that is dug straight into the earth itself. It stretches for 150 miles from north to south, similar to how the border between England and Wales sits today. At the time it was created, it was around 2.5 metres deep, and up to around 20m wide. Today, it does not represent any official boundary, but it is regarded as an important ancient monument in British history.

This image shows the boundary off Offa's Dyke (the darker line) compared to the modern boundary between England and Wales (the white line).

Offa continued taking steps like these to secure and increase the amount of land he was in charge of. Offa was so successful that at the time of his death in 796, he ruled over the largest single kingdom the Anglo-Saxon period ever saw. As the most powerful ruler in England, he declared himself 'the King of all the English', although this was never really the case.

However, Offa did do many things befitting of an all-powerful king. For example, he moved to take control of the church in England, and even made trade deals with European kings as their equals. Of course, both of these roles were things that we associated with kings and queens for centuries.

Also, he is remembered for the coins that he ordered to be produced for use during his reign. They were intricately designed and of high quality, bearing his name and image. Also, Cynethryth, Queen of

Mercia (and Offa's wife) is the only Anglo-Saxon queen whose face ever appeared on a coin (see below).

When Offa died in 796, he left a very different Mercia and England to the one he took charge of. He put Mercia in a very strong position, although there was some instability after his death. His heir, Ecgfrith, was king for less than a year, murdered by rivals.

King Egbert of Wessex

We've talked about Mercia, so we'll now turn to look at another of the major Anglo-Saxon kingdoms in the 9th Century – Wessex, and an important king of theirs, Egbert.

Egbert came to power in 802, which meant that the borders of the kingdoms in England were as seen on the map on page 59. As you'll notice, Wessex was already a major kingdom in the South of England, taking up huge areas of the South West. However, Egbert would grow this even further, and turn Wessex into Mercia's biggest challenger over who had the top kingdom in the country. This was probably helped by the fact that King Offa of Mercia had died soon before Egbert came to power.

The first years of Egbert's reign seem to have been spent resisting the growth of Mercian power in England – Mercia wanted to take over as much land in the South as they possibly could. However, Egbert was able to stand firm, stopping Mercia from taking any Wessex land.

Having managed to achieve this, Egbert must have felt that he was well organised and strong enough to go on the attack! In the year 825, he faced the Mercian king Beornwulf in a great battle at Ellendun, which is now called Wroughton. This battle was to decide who would become the dominant force in England at the time.

As it happened, Egbert won a huge victory, which allowed Wessex to take control of Essex, Sussex, and Kent. Also in this year, the East Anglians were able to drive out the Mercians, and asked Egbert for protection. Egbert would soon become king of the whole of the South of England.

While this was impressive, Egbert did not stop there!

Between the years 825 and 829, Egbert continued increasing his land and power. This eventually meant invading Mercia itself, which was also successful. Egbert now ruled Mercia, East Anglia, Essex, Kent, and Sussex, including his naïve Wessex. Intimidated, Northumbria soon submitted as well!

All this meant that Egbert achieved what no previous king had in the Anglo-Saxon era – he was in control of nearly the whole of England. As a result, the Venerable Bede named him 'Bretwalda', which either meant 'wide ruler' or even 'ruler of Britain'.

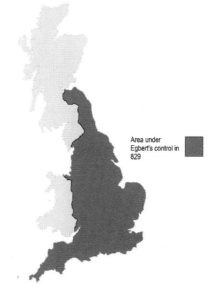

Area under Egbert's control in 829

However, Egbert would not be able to hold on to this position for very long, only holding on to this much land for around a year. Still, by the time Egbert died in the year 839, he had cemented Wessex's position as the most powerful Anglo-Saxon kingdom in the 9th century and beyond.

Question Time!

QUESTION 1

What do we mean when we say 'archaeological evidence'?

_____

_____

QUESTION 2

Using the bullet points below, write down three things that Anglo-Saxon children would do instead of going to school:

* _____

* _____

* _____

QUESTION 3

Why was it a good idea for Anglo-Saxon kings to have a loyal group of soldiers close to them?

_____

_____

_____

_____

QUESTION 4

Look at the drawing of the Anglo-Saxon below. Do you think that he looks more like a poor person or more like a king? Explain your decision.

_____

_____

_____

_____

_____

_____

QUESTION 5

Using the words in the box below, fill the gaps in the paragraph underneath. Only use each word once!

```
                                    crafting
                    warriors
        mead
                              epic
        writing
```

Anglo-Saxons were great at _____, making jewellery and decorating weapons. In a similarly creative vein, Anglo-Saxons loved to tell stories. This would both be done in _____, and through spoken word. Storytelling would take place in Great Halls, where bards would tell _____ stories of great _____. Listeners would enjoy such tales over a drink of _____ or two!

QUESTION 6

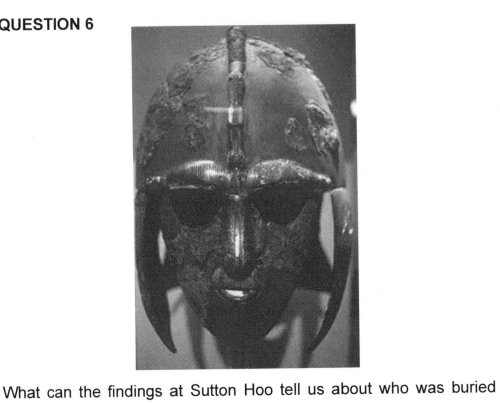

What can the findings at Sutton Hoo tell us about who was buried there?

_____

_____

_____

_____

QUESTION 7

King Offa of Mercia came into power in the year 757. Why was Mercia in a strong position to become more powerful even before it began doing so?

_____

_____

_____

_____

QUESTION 8

Why can we say that Egbert of Wessex was the most successful Anglo-Saxon king England had ever seen (at his time)?

_____

_____

_____

_____

Answers

QUESTION 1

'Archaeological evidence' refers to ancient remains that can tell us many things about the time period the items come from.

QUESTION 2

Three things that Anglo-Saxon children did instead of going to school:

- Herd cattle;
- Plant vegetables;
- Look out for wolves.

QUESTION 3

It was a good idea for Anglo-Saxon kings to have a loyal group of soldiers close to them in order to protect them. There were frequent wars over land and wealth, and killing a king was a sure way to show yourself to be the dominant force. So, it was a good idea for the king to have a security team!

QUESTION 4

The Anglo-Saxon in the drawing looks more like a king than a poor person. This is due to the fact that he is holding a large and impressive sword, and wearing a decorative helmet. These items were expensive to make, so while being useful items in their own right, they were definitely status symbols as well.

QUESTION 5

Anglo-Saxons were great at **crafting**, making jewellery and decorating weapons. In a similarly creative vein, Anglo-Saxons loved to tell stories. This would both be done in **writing**, and through spoken word. Storytelling would take place in Great Halls, where bards would tell **epic** stories of great **warriors**. Listeners would enjoy such tales over a drink of **mead** or two!

QUESTION 6

The findings at Sutton Hoo tell us that an incredibly rich and powerful person was buried there. The sheer amount of wealth in the grave shows that the person was probably a king, who wanted his money and status to accompany him to the afterlife. Of course, a poor person would not have received such a burial, and would never have seen such wealth in their whole lives.

QUESTION 7

Mercia was in a strong position to increase its power because it was already a large kingdom that was located right in the centre of England. This meant that it could expand easily into any area of England if they fortified themselves well enough.

QUESTION 8

During his reign, Egbert of Wessex was the most successful Anglo-Saxon king in history. This was because at the peak of his powers, he ruled over near enough the entirety of England. It is for this reason that the Venerable Bede named him as being 'wide ruler' or 'Britain ruler'.

HOW ARE YOU GETTING ON?

ENTER THE VIKINGS

ENTER THE VIKINGS

As we have looked at, the Anglo-Saxons seemed to love fighting each other – it happened nearly all the time for hundreds of years. However, it looked like that around the 9th and 10th centuries they would have to band together and face a common, foreign enemy. This enemy came from Scandinavia, and soon became notorious for their vicious raids up and down the British Isles. The Vikings had arrived, and the Anglo-Saxons were in serious trouble.

Who were the Vikings?

Viking settlers

How did the Anglo-Saxons cope?

The first Viking raids in Britain

You Anglo-Saxons seem to be doing well!

Meet our feared Viking plunderer, Torvald!

WHO WERE THE VIKINGS?

The Vikings have become notorious figures in English history for their legendary ruthlessness and brutality when it came to invading the Anglo-Saxons. However, it is important to note that this is not all they did – they were also traders and builders.

More peaceful Scandinavians came to settle in Britain due to the warmer climate and fertile farmland, and even mixed with the Anglo-Saxons in the 8th Century. These Vikings brought their own style of construction to Britain, and were excellent craftsmen.

They travelled the seas to Britain either to find somewhere to live, or to find goods to buy to bring back to their homes.

Ornate Viking wood carving of a wolf

However, it is much more interesting to read about the pillaging pirates that were the aggressive Vikings! These travellers were much less friendly; they were warriors, who sought glory, fame, and fortune.

Viking warriors travelled in huge boats called longships, which at the time were the most impressive ships humans had ever created. They came to England to steal and kill – the word 'Viking' may actually mean 'invader' or 'raider' in Old Norse, the language of the Scandinavians at this time.

These bandits ransacked monasteries, stealing jewels and gold from defenceless monks! The Vikings and the Anglo-Saxons did not share the same religion, meaning that the northern invaders did not care that the monasteries were sacred places for the people they were 'visiting'.

Eventually, the Vikings were even able to go further, and take some English land for themselves!

Viking Beliefs

The religions of the Anglo-Saxons and the Vikings were hugely different. While the Britons had adopted Christianity, the Vikings were pagans who worshipped many gods and goddesses, and believed that the world in which humans and animals lived was just one of nine! See below for a summary of some of their most important gods.

> The Anglo-Saxons thought of the Vikings as backwards savages for their different religions. However, the Vikings would eventually convert to Christianity as well.

Odin: The father of all gods. Odin was said to have endless wisdom, and was a god of poetry, art, and magic. However, he is a complicated figure: Odin also represented war, and often set people against each other in battle for his own amusement. He rode an 8-legged horse called Sleipnir (*the one who slides*).

Thor: A more straightforward noble god. Thor was the thunder god, who wielded an unstoppable hammer called Lightning. This god protected the human world from giants and monsters, and helped the humans grow crops and be healthy.

Loki: The trickster and 'evil' god, culprit of many crimes against gods and humans alike. Loki could shapeshift, an ability he used in his schemes and murder plots against others. He sometimes did these bad things just to make himself laugh.

Hel: The giantess ruler of Helheim, or Norse hell. Hel was Loki's daughter, and was charged with looking after those condemned to the underworld. She was said to look like one half of her face was dead, and the other side was alive. Hel was capable of bringing plague and death to whole towns.

How did the Vikings fight?

Like the Anglo-Saxons, the Vikings used simple but effective weapons and shields. They would sail up to British coasts in huge numbers, and overwhelm Anglo-Saxons with their bravery and ruthlessness. During the first attacks, English fighters had no defences in place, so they had very little chance of fending off such aggressive invaders. Later, they would take steps to change this, which we will look at soon!

Viking battle-axes were very light, and very sharp. The long shaft allowed the warrior to strike from a distance. The axe blade was often decorated with gold or silver.

Viking helmets were made from iron, and many provided protection for the eyes and nose. Most did not actually have horns!

Viking shields were big and round, and made of wood. Vikings often decorated their shields with intricate patterns, family crests or mythological figures.

In addition to the equipment shown above, raiding Vikings would wear leather shoes and armour. However, only the richest and most powerful Vikings would have swords, as they were the only ones who could afford to buy anything with such a large amount of iron.

Viking Longships

Vikings were the masters of sea travel. They were extremely comfortable on the water, using ships for travel, to fish, and to attack.

The most famous of their ships were the Viking longships, which were sometimes called dragon-ships, named after the wooden figureheads some chose to install on the front of their ships. These figureheads were probably added to scare enemies and to mark themselves out. They were also said to ward off sea monsters!

The ships themselves would be between 20 and 30 metres long, and able to hold between 40 and 60 men. Despite their size, the Vikings tried to make the ships as light as possible, so they could move them around quickly when they landed. This also meant that they could get off and onto them as fast as possible, to make surprise attacks as easy as possible!

A fjord: a river-like channel carved into land by ice.

Another important feature of the longships was that they were flat-bottomed – their undersides did not plunge deep into the ocean. This meant that they could sail in very shallow water, such as the Scandinavian fjords and the Anglo-Saxons' rivers. Think about how useful it was for the Vikings to be able to sail across the sea and all the way down a river, right into the heart of an opponent's city!

A Viking Longship

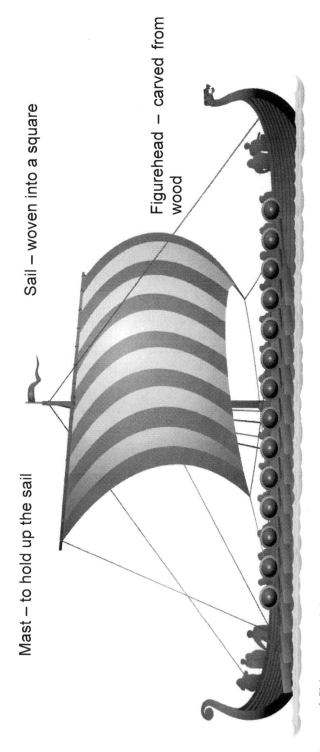

Sail – woven into a square

Figurehead – carved from wood

Mast – to hold up the sail

Oars – Vikings would row when there was no wind

THE FIRST VIKINGS RAIDS IN ENGLAND

We know that the first raid planned by the Vikings was in the year 793, on the tiny island of Lindisfarne, which is located off the coast of north-east England. Here, the Vikings targeted an undefended Christian monastery, which was packed full of Anglo-Saxon gold. Vikings will have seen these isolated but impressive buildings from sea, and been tempted to pay them a visit.

The raid itself was very one-sided, and over quickly. Vikings sailed up to the coast on which the monastery stood, and quickly overran the whole area. Several monks were murdered; blood was even spilt inside the monastery itself. Other monks were captured and taken back to Scandinavia as slaves.

The Vikings' aim was to get rich from this raid, and they succeeded. Valuable religious items (like crosses and candlesticks) made of gold and silver were all seized. Gold coins, china plates, and ornate books were also stolen by the rampant Vikings. They did not even stop there – the Vikings destroyed half the monastery by burning it down just before leaving.

Unsurprisingly, the Anglo-Saxons were horrified by this attack, the church even said that it had come as a result of the sin in people's lives. The Vikings had scared people in Britain so much that they thought the Vikings represented a punishment from God!

The Vikings continued to raid coastal areas of Britain and Ireland, and plundered monastery after monastery. As previously mentioned, the Anglo-Saxons did not have an answer to this assault, so people living on the coast were subject to unopposed raids for decades. During this time, Vikings were wary of attacking anywhere far inland, for fear of being outnumbered by Anglo-Saxon soldiers.

The Vikings' plans were simple but effective: arrive in Britain in the spring, take as many valuables as they could carry, and sail home at the end of the summer. What methods Anglo-Saxons did take rarely worked. Eventually, they even began bribing Vikings, paying them huge amounts of money to try to prevent bloodshed.

However, this did not work; the Vikings were fond of taking this bribe money with no intention of stopping. One particularly disastrous king, Ethelred the Unready, once paid a Viking leader thousands of gold coins to make him go away. The leader took the money, but continued to raid and kill, making a mockery of the agreement they had reached.

HOW DID THE ANGLO-SAXONS COPE?

Clearly, the Viking raids caused the Anglo-Saxons serious problems for long periods of time. They had to better equip themselves for defence. Enter Alfred the Great. This famous Wessexian king was not only responsible for ordering the creation of the Anglo-Saxon Chronicle (page 55), he also was an extremely important figure in terms of defending against Viking raids.

By the time Alfred rose to power around the year 870, the Vikings had been carrying out raids on England for decades. Clearly, English kings had not been successful in keeping the Vikings at bay during this time.

Anglo-Saxon rulers had failed to defeat the Vikings in battle, had no answer for their sea attacks and even tried bribing them. Alfred will have known this, realising that he needed a unique plan of his own to protect his kingdom and country. This plan seemed to involve three main tactics: Alfred wanted to better reorganise his army, he wanted to pay the Vikings to stop, and he wanted to build defensive buildings.

So, Alfred ordered the construction of several of these defensive buildings, called **burhs**, across England. Many of them were built in coastal areas, to fortify the areas of Britain the Vikings would attack first!

Anglo-Saxon Burhs

Burhs were like small towns, protected by high walls and ditches to keep what was inside safe. At first, burhs were mainly just where soldiers could stay, and keep close to areas that were commonly attacked.

In total, 33 burhs were constructed across the south of England, including one in Alfred's capital, Winchester. Over time, most of these burhs developed into towns and cities that still exist today. This is not surprising, because many of the burhs were large and all were well-protected. Also, many were built on the foundations of old Roman buildings, which had marked out major towns in the past.

All of this meant that many important Anglo-Saxon buildings were moved and kept in these burhs, as the Vikings couldn't destroy them or steal from them!

VIKING SETTLERS

Amongst all the raiding and plundering, more and more Vikings began to decide that they wanted to stop just visiting the British Isles, and start living there permanently. At first, it was only small numbers who began to do this, in remote areas out of Anglo-Saxon control, such as in Orkney, northern Scotland.

However, the Vikings eventually decided that they wanted more. Towards the end of the 9th century, they began campaigns to take land in the Anglo-Saxon kingdoms themselves. The Vikings knew they would have to go to war against leaders like King Alfred to take this land, but they weren't short of confidence.

The Anglo-Saxons called this new Viking force 'The Great Heathen Army'. It was led by a fierce Viking called Guthrum.

Despite the new measures made by Alfred the Great, such as the burhs, savage Viking attacks across England continued for years. It was an incredibly dangerous time in Anglo-Saxon England.

King Alfred, as the most powerful and important King in England at the time, had an incredibly difficult job on his hands to deal with this. Around the year 880, he and his Wessexian army suffered a serious defeat at the hands of the Great Heathen Army. The result meant that Alfred was forced to retreat to the West Country, meaning the Vikings had managed to take parts of Eastern England under their control.

However, Alfred did not earn the nickname 'The Great' for nothing – he soon rallied his troops and responded. Alfred and his soldiers rode to Edington (located in Wiltshire) to meet Guthrum and his great army. After some very hard fighting, Alfred and his Wessexians emerged victorious. Many Vikings were killed, and those who survived were forced to retreat.

Following this, Alfred actually got the Vikings to agree to a peace deal. This deal even involved Guthrum becoming a Christian. However, the Viking king did not stick to the treaty. The two sides quickly began fighting again.

So, Alfred was forced to modernise and reorganise. For example, he ordered his own version of the longship to be built, assembling a fleet to take on the Vikings at sea. This also involved building more burhs and making sure they were always occupied by a full-time army. Fighting continued like this for several years.

During all this time, despite the huge challenges he was faced with, Alfred was strongly committed to improving the quality of life of people in Anglo-Saxon England. For example, he was hugely in favour of children having access to education, and took many steps to promote literacy in English, which had been massively disrupted during Viking raids. He also changed the legal system, writing down many official laws that he introduced in England. It's for these reasons, as well as his dealings with the Vikings, that he is loved even up to this day.

He also did eventually manage to get the Vikings to accept and honour a second peace deal – one that would change the face of Anglo-Saxon history forever.

The Danelaw

This second agreement between Alfred the Great of the Anglo-Saxons and Guthrum of the Vikings would be all to do with the creation of the Danelaw.

Basically, Alfred knew that if he wanted to stop the Viking onslaught, he would have to give them something they really wanted; not just money which they could easily steal. So, he decided to arrange a deal that would see the Vikings be given huge amounts of Anglo-Saxon land.

So, England was divided up in to two kingdoms: Anglo-Saxon England and the Danelaw. See a map below to see how the new map of England would have looked. You'll notice that the Vikings were actually given a bigger chunk of land – Alfred wanted to make them really happy. This split in England would last for decades.

The Danelaw

Anglo-Saxon England

While this agreement aimed to bring peace to England, it did not entirely work! Raids continued to be carried out across the border by both sides, so fighting went on for years.

So, the Anglo-Saxons had had to give up around half of their land to survive. Life continued about as normally as it could for them with their reduced power. However, people's lives in the newly-created Danelaw changed massively.

Life in the Danelaw

Of course, people in the Danelaw lived a Viking way of life. This was surprisingly similar to an Anglo-Saxon way of life; they lived, conducted law, and worked as the early Anglo-Saxons did. The only major differences had to do with language and religion.

For the Anglo-Saxons, the divide made them realise that their own differences were not as important as they were during the many years of fighting between their kingdoms. The result of this was that Anglo-Saxons were beginning to move away from seeing themselves as being 'Wessexian' or 'Mercian', and towards seeing themselves as 'English'. They were coming together as one people.

Having said this, the differences between the Anglo-Saxons and the Vikings also became less and less important as time went on. By the time the Vikings had been living in England for around 20 years, Viking and Anglo-Saxon people had begun to mix. Trade was conducted between the two sides, common stories were told, and children were born with family history on both sides of the Danelaw. While Anglo-Saxon England and the Danelaw were far from being peacefully united, change had begun to take place.

Unsurprisingly, however, this did not continue peacefully.

King Athelstan

A few decades after the Danelaw was created, Alfred the Great was dead and his grandson had the throne. This new ruler was called Athelstan.

Athelstan's reign is best remembered for his efforts to take back English land from the Vikings, and for effectively bringing about an end to the Danelaw. During this time, people living in England were starting to see themselves as belonging to a wider nation – Alfred arguably invented the concept of 'Englishness'. After the end of the Danelaw, people of Viking descent in Britain would start to identify themselves as English.

Athelstan is one of the first figures in British history whose main priority was uniting the island to become one nation. Of course, he faced lots of opposition, and not only from the Vikings, who wanted to keep control of their own state (the Danelaw). Another group of people standing in Athelstan's way was the Scots.

From around the time of Alfred the Great, people in Scotland had been gradually uniting under King Constantine II (the second). They too had developed nationalist feelings (loyalty to a country), and wanted more land, just as Athelstan did. So, this meant that huge chunks of northern England were wanted by both kings. As if this wasn't bad enough, much of this land belonged to the Vikings, who did not want to give it up!

The only thing that was certain was that the 10th century (between the years 900 and 999) was going to see lots of fighting and death.

From around the year 920 to the year 940, all three forces were involved with fighting each other, with the Vikings often dealing with two attacks at once. With the English attacking them from the south and the Scottish doing so from the north, the Vikings found themselves trapped between the two British kings.

The Danelaw's capital falls

In the year 927, Athelstan and his troops set about taking back the city of York from the Vikings. This was a daunting task, as York (which the Vikings called Jorvik) was a major city. You can look at it as being like the capital of the Danelaw. However, Athelstan actually managed to take it with relative ease. It is said that he took advantage of the death of the Viking ruler of York to achieve this – they were too weak to attack during this moment of instability.

Of course, this meant that the boundaries between the Danelaw and Anglo-Saxon England were becoming less and less clear. While this was what Athelstan wanted, it created chaos. He also had the Scots to deal with…

Athelstan vs. Constantine

Up until the year 937, fighting between the English and the Scots had not provided a clear winner. Athelstan and Constantine were both distracted by the Vikings, so both sides were unable to commit to an open battle with their full power.

However, in the year 937, such a battle finally took place. Both kings were able to prepare as well as they could and assemble massive armies. Athelstan convinced many of the historically powerful Anglo-Saxons to join him, while Constantine recruited many Viking leaders to lend a hand.

These gatherings of armies had lasting consequences for people in England. For example, Athelstan's success in recruiting many different Anglo-Saxon noblemen led to the English uniting as one. At the same time, Constantine's alliance with the Vikings sped up the process by which they were mixing with people in Britain.

However, this fight was to be extremely bloody, and represent the climax of the feud between the English and the Scots. In other words, it was to decide who would become the most powerful group in England. It was called the battle of Brunanburh.

The Battle of Brunanburh – 937

While it is impossible to know many of the key events of the battle, we can understand that there was a huge loss of life. The Anglo-Saxon Chronicle calls this battle the greatest slaughter ever seen in Britain.

Many important and powerful figures from both sides were killed, but one side did claim victory – Athelstan and the English.

As such, they were able to maintain their control across England, while Constantine was forced to flee back to Scotland. However, the English losses were so great that they did not make as many land gains as they may have wanted.

Following this great battle Athelstan became the most powerful man in Britain. His victory had led many to label him as the first king of a united England.

The End of the Danelaw

As you can tell from the section about Athelstan, the Vikings were becoming less and less powerful in England. This was partly because they were mixing with the English and Scottish – they were no longer the feared foreign barbarian. Over the decades the Scandinavians had been settling in Britain, the differences between the Vikings and Anglo-Saxons became much less striking.

The Vikings' loss of power is also related to the Anglo-Saxons uniting as one, and becoming stronger as a result. Descendants of Vikings would eventually buy into this notion, and come to identify themselves as 'English'.

All of these ingredients eventually led to the end of the Danelaw. This did not mean that all Vikings and descendants of Vikings left England; rather that the country was no longer split into two kingdoms.

Of course, this change was not a peaceful one!

Fighting continued over the Viking-controlled areas of Northumbria (which they still had after the Battle of Brunanburh) until around the year 954. It was in this year that Eric Bloodaxe, the Viking in power in this area, was killed and the Anglo-Saxons could take full control. After this, the Vikings in England and the Anglo-Saxons began to fully mix with one another.

The death of Eric Bloodaxe spelt the end of the Danelaw, and brought about the clearest image of a united England yet. Although now ruled by one people, England was still a very diverse and often chaotic place to live.

Question Time!

QUESTION 1

Below is a collection of possible reasons the Vikings had for invading England. Circle all the ones you think are correct!

> To take land   To steal gold
>
> They were bored
>
> For better weather
>
> They hated the English

QUESTION 2

Why did the Vikings not care about destroying monasteries or killing monks?

_____

_____

_____

QUESTION 3

Write a short description for the Norse God Thor.

_____

_____

_____

_____

_____

_____

QUESTION 4

Why were the Vikings such good fighters?

_____

_____

_____

_____

_____

_____

_____

QUESTION 5

After the first Viking raids, which horrified the Anglo-Saxons, what did the church say had caused them?

_____

_____

_____

QUESTION 6

In the boxes below, write down three steps Alfred the Great took to protect England from the Viking invaders.

Explain them in the space below:

1. _____

_____

_____

2. _____

_____

_____

3. _____

_____

_____

QUESTION 7

How did the Battle of Brunanburh help bring the English together as a group, as well as help bring the Scottish together as a group?

_____

_____

_____

_____

QUESTION 8

What happened after the death of Viking Eric Bloodaxe in the year 954?

_____

_____

_____

_____

Answers

QUESTION 1

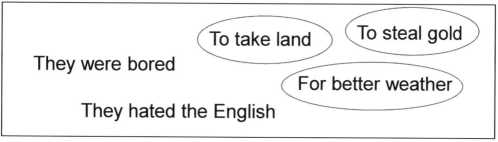

They were bored

To take land

To steal gold

For better weather

They hated the English

QUESTION 2

The Vikings did not care about destroying monasteries or killing monks because they were not yet Christians. The British would have seen this as a huge violation because of their Christianity – it was like an attack on their God.

QUESTION 3

Thor was a thunder god, who had a huge hammer that could control lightening. Thor protected the human world from giants and monsters from other worlds, and was also associated with health – worshipping Thor brought good luck to farmers.

QUESTION 4

The main reason that Vikings were such good fighters was due to their sheer ruthlessness and bravery. They would fully commit to their leaders, and were experts in using their simple but effective weaponry. Vikings also had a secret weapon – their longships could sail down rivers and right into the heart of Anglo-Saxon towns.

QUESTION 5

The church blamed the horrific scenes caused by the Viking attacks on the Anglo-Saxons' supposed lack of commitment to God.

QUESTION 6

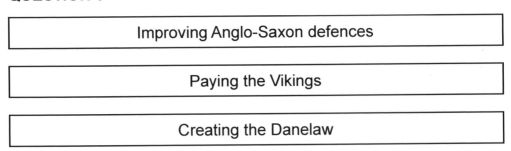

Improving Anglo-Saxon defences

Paying the Vikings

Creating the Danelaw

1. Alfred the Great knew that he needed to improve the systems of defence that Britain had. To this end, he constructed burhs, brought in a permanent anti-Viking army, and even built longships to compete with the Vikings on the water.

2. Alfred will have known that paying the Vikings to leave England alone had not worked in the past. However, he knew that doing so would buy him time to make the preparations he wanted to in order to keep England safe.

3. The most extreme measure Alfred took was signing huge areas of England over to the Vikings, creating the Danelaw region of England. Potentially, this saved England from falling completely into the Vikings' hands, who were advancing ruthlessly until this point.

QUESTION 7

The Battle of Brunanburh helped bring the English together as one group because it made the Anglo-Saxons united against a common enemy – the Scottish. This was important as the Anglo-Saxon era had been marked by near-constant fighting between the kingdoms. Similarly, the Scottish came together for this event as well, and really began to embrace a sense of nationality.

QUESTION 8

The death of Eric Bloodaxe meant that the Vikings had failed to hold on to their land as stated by the Danelaw. So, The Anglo-Saxons were able to reclaim this land, meaning the era of the Danelaw came to an end.

THE END OF THE ANGLO-SAXON ERA

THE END OF THE ANGLO-SAXON ERA

As you have seen, the Anglo-Saxons managed to keep control of England for hundreds of years, and overcame many grave challenges in the process. However, the Anglo-Saxon era did eventually come to an end. What's surprising though, is that it was not the Vikings who were the main cause of it! This final chapter will cover the events of the final years of Anglo-Saxon England, and what came after it.

Ethelred the Unready

Britain in chaos

King Canute

We had a good run...

To talk you through the end of his era, here is King Athelstan!

ETHELRED THE UNREADY

Ethelred the Unready

In 980 Vikings started to raid the English coast again. During the time of these new raids, England was being ruled by King Ethelred. Ethelred has since been given the nickname 'the Unready', for his famously disastrous dealings with the new Viking invaders.

> What went so wrong for him?

These new raids were unexpected – England had not had to deal with foreign invasions for several decades. Although there had been lots of fighting on British land during these years, the English were out of practice when it came to defending themselves from sea attacks.

To make it worse, the defences that the Anglo-Saxons had built on their coasts during the first set of Viking raids had not been looked after, and were falling apart. Clearly, England was wholly unprepared to deal with the ruthless Vikings, who were expert raiders at this point.

As a result, many cities and towns across the south coast of England were stripped of their wealth with ease. Ethelred and his armies struggled to deal with this, so the invaders started taking cities for their own. The Vikings wanted to own English land once more.

The Battle of Maldon

This battle represents the major clash between English and Viking forces at this time. The legend goes that the Vikings met the great English warrior Byrhtnoth on the Thames Estuary, with both their armies facing each other off across the water.

The English were greatly outnumbered, but did not back down. So, when fighting started, many English were killed – it was a clear Viking victory. Despite this, Byrhtnoth's bravery in this situation caused him to be remembered as an English hero. We know this because there was an epic poem written about this event, praising Byrhtnoth for his actions. Clearly, courage in the face of death was still something that was very highly respected.

So, what did Ethelred do next?

Desperate for a solution, Ethelred started doing what so many had done before him – bribe the Vikings for peace. This was a huge mistake – it had never worked in the past!

The idea of paying Vikings to stop them attacking was called 'Danegeld'.

Ethelred could only watch as more and more of his land and people were taken over by Viking raiders. He wanted a quick solution, and he knew that offering Danegeld was an option. He also would have thought about the fact that England had recently become very rich. All the while, however, he will have known that accepting money had not stopped the Vikings in the past.

Despite everything, Ethelred decided to pay the Vikings the largest offering of Danegeld ever seen in England, hoping that the Vikings would be satisfied and stop attacking. In the end, he paid the invading raiders around a million pounds' worth of silver to go away. They didn't.

Of course, this was an absolute disaster for England and its people. It was an incredible amount of money to offer to an enemy for peace, and it didn't even work! Taxpayers had to contribute to this offering, so people were essentially paying the wages of the soldiers who were killing them.

Ethelred needed a different solution, and he needed it quickly.

Following the disastrous Danegeld, Ethelred completely lost control. By this point, he had completely failed to protect his country from the new Viking raiders, and had even paid them for the pleasure of their visit. If he had been desperate before, he was completely panicking now.

In November of the year 1002, Ethelred, King of England, ordered the murder of all Viking men in England, as well as anyone of Viking descent. Many deaths are thought to have occurred during this event, which is called the St. Brice's Day Massacre.

This was a terrible mistake by Ethelred. Not only was it cruel to murder hundreds of innocents, but he had ordered the deaths of his own people by including English dwellers of Viking descent. Many of those killed are believed to be people who were born in England and had shown nothing but loyalty to English rule. This turned many people against him.

Unsurprisingly, Viking leaders in Scandinavia were incredibly angry at this event, and swore revenge. Ethelred had hoped to eliminate the threat of Viking invasions, but in ordering the St. Brice's Day Massacre he made it much worse.

A Viking King of England?

The St. Brice's Day Massacre set off a chain of events that would change the face of English history. For Ethelred the Unready, it was going to be a complete disaster.

What can you see happening in England at this point?

Vikings in Scandinavia wanted revenge, and prepared for a huge invasion of England. This would have also been motivated by gold; the Vikings still wanted to make money.

The attack was to be led by Sweyn Forkbeard, a powerful king. Legend has it that Sweyn's sister, a noblewoman called Gunhilde, was killed in the massacre.

It is thought that another reason that Sweyn invaded at this time was because he wanted to become King of England, and saw a chance to do so with Ethelred in a weak position. In any case, what is certain is that Sweyn Forkbeard was preparing to commit to a large-scale invasion of England.

The Viking offensive

In the year 1003, only a few months after the St Brice's Day Massacre, Sweyn Forkbeard and his Viking troops landed in Britain. There were several years of raids and fighting between the English and the Vikings, with the Vikings slowly gaining a foothold in England as time went on. The English even started paying more Danegeld!

This war continued for about 10 years. During this time, Ethelred paid Sweyn even more than he had paid the new raiders in the year 980! This had a devastating effect on people's lives as Britain was becoming very poor.

In addition, the people in England were becoming more and more scared and unhappy. As word spread of Viking attacks, people started fleeing their homes; they had no faith that their king was protecting them.

All the while, Sweyn was conquering land and becoming more influential. By the year 1013, he had taken control of many major English cities, and was closing in on London where Ethelred himself was hiding. This was looking like the end of 'the Unready King'.

KING CANUTE

The climax of these events was to be rather messy and complicated. In 1013, knowing that Sweyn Forkbeard was closing in on him, Ethelred fled to Normandy in France with his family. His wife, Emma, was the Duke of Normandy's daughter so he knew he would be safe there. Another thing that made him flee was the fact that he had lost the trust of his advisors, as well as the English people as a whole.

This meant that Sweyn could take the kingdom for himself; no one dared oppose him. He had conquered the whole of the country, becoming the first ever Viking king of England. However, his rule was only to last a few weeks, because he died suddenly! It is thought that this was due to illness, but some believe that it was more suspicious than that...

This plunged England into even more chaos. Sweyn's son, Canute, was lined up to replace him, but it would not be that simple. News of Sweyn's death reached Ethelred, who saw it as a chance to reclaim power. He returned to England, where the noblemen (who had let Sweyn take power) decided to swear loyalty to Ethelred once again.

Canute, not wanting to risk another long war so soon, conceded and sailed back home to Scandinavia, specifically Denmark. Amazingly, Ethelred found himself ruling England once more, despite the series of errors that had come to define his kingship.

Canute comes back

As it turned out, Canute decided to leave England in order to reorganise and build up a new fighting force of his own. So, in the year 1015, he arrived back in Britain with a huge army of Vikings from all over Scandinavia. It was clear that he was not here simply to raid – he wanted the English crown that was once his father's, as well as all the land, glory, and riches that came with it. He was a very strong leader, and came to be nicknamed 'the Great'.

This new war went on for over a year.

Ethelred was about 50 years old at the time of Canute's invasion, and actually died soon after – during the first half of 1016. His son, Edmund, then became leader of the English forces, and king by default. The new

King Edmund was nicknamed 'Ironside' due to his incredible ability on the battlefield.

So, the war in England then became a straight fight between Edmund Ironside and Canute the Great for the Kingdom of England. In 1016, a long summer of fighting took place in which Canute was able to take control of most of England, despite Edmund's brave and tough last stand. Despite this defeat, Edmund was able to keep control of parts of the south east of England, on condition that he did not challenge the Vikings for the rest of the country.

Canute and his Viking empire

However, the English were not able to keep hold of this last piece of land for very long. Edmund died at the end of 1016, only months after he had become king. It is believed that he was murdered, although (strangely) it probably wasn't Canute who was to blame. As a result, Edmund's death is shrouded in mystery.

In any case, Canute the Great could then take over the last parts of England that were not already his, and become king. He moved to strengthen his position and minimise the chances of any further war or challenge to his power. In a tactical move, Canute even married Ethelred the Unready's widow, Emma, in order to make the people of England more likely to accept him.

His success in achieving this meant that he became a successful and even popular king – he made sure that his reign was peaceful for his subjects. Also, Canute was now ruler of England as well as huge sections of Scandinavia that he already controlled. This is why we can say that he was the leader of a Viking empire.

In the end, Canute ruled for around 20 years, dying in the year 1035. Unfortunately, this event was going to plunge England into chaos once more – a new fight for the throne was about to begin.

The years following the death of King Canute were complicated, because several people believed that they were the rightful heir to the throne. So, there were many arguments and a lot of fighting over who would rule England. There were four main challengers.

Two of Ethelred the Unready and Emma's sons, Edward and Alfred, believed they had claim to the throne. They were also competing with Canute and Emma's son, Harthacnut, as well as Canute's son born during his first marriage, Harold.

This was a messy situation, don't worry if you find it difficult to get to grips with!

In the end, a few of these challengers ended up taking the throne at one point or another, and none of them did so for very long. Look at the timeline below for a summary of how power changed hands in England between the years 1035 and 1042.

BRITAIN IN CHAOS

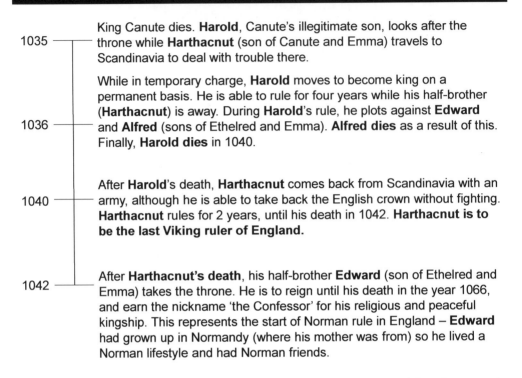

1035 — King Canute dies. **Harold**, Canute's illegitimate son, looks after the throne while **Harthacnut** (son of Canute and Emma) travels to Scandinavia to deal with trouble there.

1036 — While in temporary charge, **Harold** moves to become king on a permanent basis. He is able to rule for four years while his half-brother (**Harthacnut**) is away. During **Harold**'s rule, he plots against **Edward** and **Alfred** (sons of Ethelred and Emma). **Alfred dies** as a result of this. Finally, **Harold dies** in 1040.

1040 — After **Harold**'s death, **Harthacnut** comes back from Scandinavia with an army, although he is able to take back the English crown without fighting. Harthacnut rules for 2 years, until his death in 1042. **Harthacnut is to be the last Viking ruler of England.**

1042 — After **Harthacnut's death**, his half-brother **Edward** (son of Ethelred and Emma) takes the throne. He is to reign until his death in the year 1066, and earn the nickname 'the Confessor' for his religious and peaceful kingship. This represents the start of Norman rule in England – **Edward** had grown up in Normandy (where his mother was from) so he lived a Norman lifestyle and had Norman friends.

So, as you have seen, lots of people from all sorts of backgrounds had wanted to rule England over the years. In the eleventh century, England had seen kings of Anglo-Saxon descent, Viking rulers, and powerful Normans. Despite this constant changing of rule, life for people living in England had remained pretty similar.

In the many wars over England, everyday citizens had lost their lives, and had been forced to pay huge amounts of tax in the process. They had no power over how they wanted their country to be run, and had to focus on their own trades and farming to survive.

Dying for your leaders in battle was still a vital part of being a soldier, so thousands were happy to lay down their lives in these constant battles for power.

Harald Hardrada

After Edward the Confessor died in 1066, there was yet another struggle for power over the English crown. This was because Edward did not have any children, so there was no clear heir to his throne. Three main challengers for the position emerged, all feeling that they deserved it. Unsurprisingly, they were willing to fight for it as well.

Among these challengers was the Viking King of Norway, Harald Hardrada. Harald had ruled this part of Scandinavia for many years, and was known for his eagerness to invade other areas in order to conquer land for his country. It is said that Harald Hardrada was the last great Viking king whose death marked the end of the Viking Era.

This is because after Harald's death, Viking raids and conquests to foreign lands became much less frequent. In fact, they had basically stopped by the end of the eleventh century. It seems that kings and people in Scandinavia wanted to focus on their own issues at home, and began to stop raiding as a result. This is something that arguably still defines the area today.

Harald's English campaign

So, soon after Edward the Confessor's death, Harald assembled an army and sailed to England, landing at Northumbria in the north east. One of his opponents for the crown, Harold Godwinson (an English nobleman) met him in battle at Stamford Bridge in Yorkshire.

This battle was an extremely brutal one, with around 10,000 people losing their lives in total. However, most of these losses were taken by the Vikings, who were defeated. Harald Hardrada was himself killed, as he was hit in the throat by an arrow. His attempt to become king of England had failed.

Who became king?

However, Harold Godwinson would not end the year with the crown either. The third challenger, William the Conqueror of Normandy, would soon defeat the Englishman during the famous Battle of Hastings. He invaded England in the south only days after Harold's battle, so he knew that Harold would not be fully prepared for him. As we know from the Bayeux Tapestry, William was then crowned King of England.

This is when England fully became a Norman country, and brought an end to both the Anglo-Saxon and Viking eras.

BAYEUX TAPESTRY.

Harold's Coronation.

Question Time!

QUESTION 1

Why was Ethelred's tactic of paying the Vikings such a disastrous one?

_____

_____

_____

QUESTION 2

Answer the following multiple choice questions about what happened in England after the St. Brice's Day Massacre.

1. Viking reaction to this event was…

   a) One of extreme anger; they swore vengeance.

   b) They were not in favour of it, but agreed it needed to happen.

   c) They were in favour of the decision.

2. In the year 1003, Sweyn Forkbeard…

   a) Made a peaceful agreement with King Ethelred.

   b) Invaded Anglo-Saxon England, aiming to conquer it.

   c) Paid Ethelred to leave the Vikings alone.

3. After Canute, Viking King of England, died in the year 1035...

a) England entered a rare time of peace.

b) The Viking Harald Hardrada became king.

c) Years of chaos eventually resulted in a Norman King of England, ending the Anglo-Saxon era.

Answers

QUESTION 1

Ethelred's tactic of paying the Vikings was such a disastrous one because it made people in Britain incredibly poor, and did not even save them from being attacked by the Vikings.

QUESTION 2

1. Viking reaction to this event was...

   a) One of extreme anger; they swore vengeance.

2. In the year 1003, Sweyn Forkbeard...

   b) Invaded Anglo-Saxon England, aiming to conquer it.

3. After Canute, Viking King of England, died in the year 1035...

   c) Years of chaos eventually resulted in a Norman King of England, ending the Anglo-Saxon era.

HOW ARE YOU GETTING ON?

PRIMARY History

Mock Paper:

The Anglo-Saxons

40 minutes

First Name	
Middle Name/s	
Last Name	
School	
Date of Birth	D D / M M / Y Y Y Y

1 In the boxes below, there are two possible answers to the question: "Why did the Angles, Saxons, and Jutes come to Britain in the first place?" Choose which one you think is best, by writing 'A' or 'B' in the box underneath.

A | The Angles, Saxons, and Jutes were trying to sail to America when they accidentally arrived in Britain. They aimed to trade their handmade goods to the Native Americans.

B | The Romano-Britons, under attack from the Picts and Scots, turned to Europe for help. King Vortigern paid the Angles, Saxons, and Jutes to come to his aid, and defeat the tribesmen from the North.

Your answer:

2 ma

2 Not all Anglo-Saxon soldiers would possess iron longswords. Why was this?

_____

_____

_____

_____

_____

3 ma

3 What led the Venerable Bede to call Egbert of Wessex 'Bretwalda'?

_____

_____

_____

_____

2 ma

4 What is the name of the huge man-made trench, created to mark a Mercian border, depicted in the map below?

1 mark

5 The Huns, including their feared leader, Attila, were painted in a devil-like light by the Romans. Why was this?

_____

_____

_____

_____

3 marks

6 Using the empty boxes, label this Anglo-Saxon soldier's battle equipment.

3 m

 7 Why do you think that Anglo-Saxons developed near-sacred bonds between soldiers and their leaders?

_____

_____

_____

_____

_____

_____

_____

4 m

8 Using the words in the box below, fill the gaps in the paragraph underneath to complete the piece of writing about the Sutton Hoo Burial.

```
        warrior

                                    boat

            rich            sword
  gold

                  heaven
```

There are many conclusions we can make about the person who was buried at Sutton Hoo. The most obvious one is that the person was very _____, as they were buried surrounded by untold wealth; _____ coins and lavish ornaments. A second conclusion we can make is that the person was a great _____ – they were buried with an impressive _____, which not all soldiers would have been able to own. Finally, the fact that this person was buried inside a _____ shows us an Anglo-Saxon view of the afterlife – whoever buried him wanted him to be prepared to sail into _____.

6 marks

9 Do you think that Alfred the Great's creation of the Danelaw saved England from being completely taken over by the Vikings? This answer is based on personal opinion – make sure you explain why you think so/think not.

_____

_____

_____

_____

5 marks

What was the St. Brice's Day Massacre? Put a tick in the box next to the correct answer.

This was a disastrous event ordered by King Ethelred the Unready involving the killing of many people of Viking origin in Anglo-Saxon England. It was a desperate response to new Viking raids.

This was a series of murders carried out by Guthrum, the Viking leader, against many high-profile Anglo-Saxons during the time of the Danelaw. It led to his arrest and exile back to Scandinavia.

This event is a shameful blemish on the reputation of Alfred the Great. It involved the execution of several of his own men who he suspected of being friends with Vikings. Modern historians don't want you to know about it.

1 n

ANSWERS

The answer is 'B' (according to Gildas). In any case, the Angles, Saxons and Jutes were definitely not trying to sail to America.

Not all Anglo-Saxon soldiers would possess iron longswords because they were incredibly expensive to make. This meant that only the richest and most powerful soldiers would be able to afford one – longswords became a symbol of status and wealth.

Egbert of Wessex was referred to as 'Bretwalda', due to the fact that he was the first king in the Anglo-Saxon era to gain control of near enough the whole of England. At the peak of his powers in the year 829, he controlled Mercia, East Anglia, Essex, Kent, Sussex, and Northumbria.

The huge man-made trench marking the Mercian border is called Offa's Dyke.

The Romans depicted the Huns, including Attila, in a devil-like light because they were scared of their ruthless fighting style. The Huns grew to become the dominant tribe in Europe around the time of the end of the Roman Empire – they arguably forced the Romans out of Western Europe.

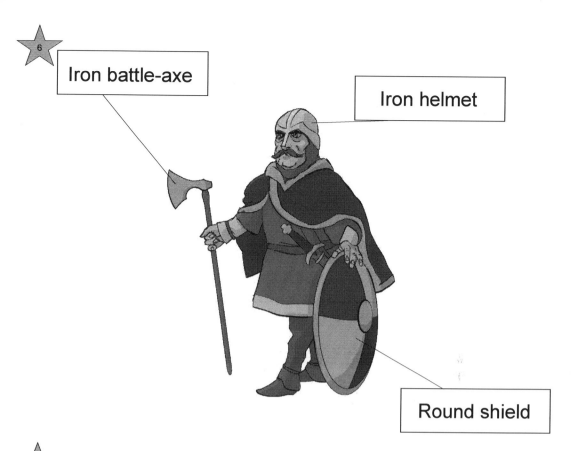

Iron battle-axe

Iron helmet

Round shield

It is possible to say that Anglo-Saxon soldiers developed near-sacred bonds with their leaders in order to give themselves the best chance to win in battle. If soldiers were fully committed, and saw bravery as being the only possible option, then they would be fighting as well as they could. This could only help leaders; tribes without this bond would have been defeated more easily.

There are many conclusions we can make about the person who was buried at Sutton Hoo. The most obvious one is that the person was very **rich**, as they were buried surrounded by untold wealth; **gold** coins and lavish ornaments. A second conclusion we can make is that the person was a great **warrior** – they were buried with an impressive **sword**, which not all soldiers would have been able to own. Finally, the fact that this person was buried inside a **boat** shows us an Anglo-Saxon view of the afterlife – whoever buried him wanted him to be prepared to sail into **heaven**.

9

(This answer is based on personal opinion, see below for a sample response. For full marks, you must have made at least 2 points and explained them.)

I think that Alfred the Great's creation of the Danelaw did save England from being completely taken over by the Vikings. The deal to split England into a Viking zone and an Anglo-Saxon zone hugely reduced the amount of people who were dying in the constant Viking raids. Alfred and his troops were at breaking point, and had to submit to the Great Heathen Army, otherwise they would have lost the rest of their land in the war that would have carried on, probably for years.

10

This was a disastrous event ordered by King Ethelred the Unready involving the killing of many people of Viking origin in Anglo-Saxon England. It was a desperate response to new Viking raids.

This was a series of murders carried out by Guthrum, the Viking leader, against many high-profile Anglo-Saxons during the time of the Danelaw. It led to his arrest and exile back to Scandinavia.

This event is a shameful blemish on the reputation of Alfred the Great. It involved the execution of several of his own men who he suspected of being friends with Vikings. Modern historians don't want you to know about it.

WANT MORE HELP WITH KS1 AND KS2 HISTORY?

CHECK OUT OUR OTHER HISTORY GUIDES:

How2Become have created other FANTASTIC guides to help you and your child learn all they need and want to for history at primary level

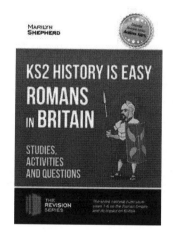
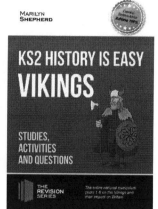
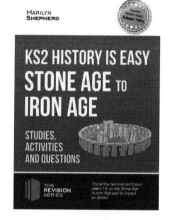

These exciting guides are filled with engaging facts and fun activities to ensure that their study is interesting, and their learning is improved! Invest in your child's future today!

FOR MORE INFORMATION ON OUR KEY STAGE 1 AND 2 (KS1 and KS2) GUIDES, PLEASE CHECK OUT THE FOLLOWING:

WWW.HOW2BECOME.COM

Get Access To

FREE

Educational Resources

www.MyPsychometricTests.co.uk

29254800R00072

Printed in Great Britain
by Amazon